WRITERS REPUBLIC

From My
Unconventional
Heart

The Little Pink Book

HAYLEY N. CHOW

WRITERS REPUBLIC L.L.C.
515 Summit Ave. Unit R1
Union City, NJ 07087, USA
Website: *www.writersrepublic.com*
Hotline: *1-877-656-6838*
Email: *info@writersrepublic.com*

Ordering Information:
Quantity sales. Special discounts are available on quantity purchases by corporations, associations, and others. For details, contact the publisher at the address above.

Library of Congress Control Number:	2021914894	
ISBN-13:	978-1-63728-554-1	[Paperback Edition]
	978-1-63728-555-8	[Hardback Edition]
	978-1-63728-556-5	[Digital Edition]

Rev. date: 08/13/2021

FOREWORD

As we look through the eyes of the persona who emerges in these writings, we see a world defined by a small number of issues, a miniature world made up of one young woman and the things that set her heart throbbing and, more often, that make it break. She is a dedicated romantic of the old school— looking for love, longing to love, baffled, pummeled, and stymied by love, habitually disappointed but never once defeated. And yes, she is a millennial, so she stands smack in the center of her own universe. Men, and women too, appear in this book, this microcosm of her creation, because of how they impact her, what they make her feel— about them and, just as often, about herself. Perception of others blends imperceptibly into self-perception, and vice versa, because it is true that we can see ourselves only through the eyes of others, and because it is also true that we project onto others what we see in ourselves.

So: the center of this book is the author's self. Yet the book does not read as self-centered. Between "I, myself, and me" (p. 18) and the reader there is always a distance, so that even as we feel at one with the person who speaks to us from these pages, we also remain aware of being apart from her. Sure, that person gets in our face sometimes, but never to the point where we stop seeing her, never to the point where we lose focus and judgment. Because on the flip side of all this self-display is the author's gentle self-irony. Because, as much as we are invited to resonate and sympathize, we are also here to learn—from, through, and together with this person.

It may be an exaggeration to say that this little collection of writings is deep. This is the work of a young writer, showing many of the limitations that it is reasonable to expect of someone who is nearer the beginning than the end of her life. And yet there is depth to this book. Beneath the overlay of the girlish flings, and the constantly dashed and eternally springing hopes of early womanhood, which make up the bulk of the matter in these pages, lies a bedrock formed from experiences of an entirely different kind. As with an iceberg, which mostly sits submerged below the surface, we get only a hint that these experiences exist. "Fitting in, I never did well / That I always knew / For I grew up quickly and aggressively / Because of everything I had been through" (p. 15) One clue, and nothing more.

It is a measure of the author's mature restraint, and the careful regard she has for her readers, that she has chosen, for now, to keep silent. Yet, even hidden from view, the parts of the life she holds back are there to shore up the parts that she does reveal to us, giving them a tensile strength, a feeling of stability. And so, for all the apparent conventionality of its subject matter, Hayley's book is an unconventional act of self-expression that comes from the heart.

Alice W. Cheang

Alice W. Cheang (B.A. Yale, Ph.D. Harvard) is a literary critic and translator of Chinese classical poetry and modern fiction.

Contents

LEARNING

'Learning' consists of true tales of expectations and growth, the harder times in life, and learning to love yourself.

Welcome

Welcome to my mess, my stress
My highs and my lows
I will now be speaking in prose
(Yeah, I'm one of those)

Grab a glass if you need one
Cheers, I'll guide you through
Notes on my experiences
Maybe even written about you

So come and escape into my world
Hopefully you can relate
If not I hope this gives you a good chuckle
About my biggest, yet fabulous mistakes

Oz

You were my childhood
You were my friend
A fantasy I wonderfully painted
It was always you in the end

Somehow along the way we got lost
Stubbornly tugging and trying to fend
It was a glorious and vibrant rainbow
But we were headed for opposite ends

Overthinking

Lately I haven't been able to hide, it seems
Not even in my rest
For my worries seem to find me
Of me they get the very best

Anxiety? Maybe. Restlessness, yes
Emotions are not my forte
This has become my punishment
For all the things I guess I repress

Waiting Room

They make it look so easy
Falling deep in love
As time passes, and years go by
I question myself of

I can't help but think I'm broken
I'm just a waiting room in the dark
Here I sit still waiting
Patiently guarding my heart

Once Upon A Time

I don't believe in regrets, the "what ifs" in life
Some memories are meant to have that "what if" factor
A perfect moment tucked away
A secret little happily ever after

The story never continued on
Never quite reached the falling action part
Simply something you can look back on fondly
A special reservation for just you and your heart

New Year's Resolution

For it has never changed
All these years while wearing that shiny dress
I wished for one single thing
That I could be the very best

No, not the popular one, not the star of a one-woman show
Not the man of my dreams, I'm not opposed to that though
The one thing I've dreamed for all of these years
Is to be the best friend I possibly can, to my incredibly loyal peers

Unexplainable

There are two things
That make my heart beat

The kind where it is unfathomable
And unimaginable

Doing what I love
And loving you

Self-Doubt

I claim I know my worth
I don't waste time to roam
So why do they sleep in pairs?
And I go home alone

Optimism

There will be that one
He will change your mind
Walls built from stone will plummet
For looking at him will remind

Reminded of the good that people possess
For it's possible and it's true
I remembered all of this once again
The very moment I first met you

The Girl Next Door

Someone I admire
Someone often sought
Someone I very much regret to inform
Someone that I'm very much not

Immaturity

Me, I tend to run
The first red flag I see
I blame them all for leaving
But is the only one leaving just me?

The Invitation

My love, he sent me a letter
With a beautiful golden wax seal
I accepted graciously
Hurried to the ball in my favorite starred heels

When the carriage arrived, something felt terribly wrong
I realized quickly I wasn't the only one
For standing next to him was a tasteless maiden
That acted as if she had already won

After the celebration, he and I had planned to meet
But she desired to interject
She cursed my name if I wouldn't allow her join
So I kindly chose to accept

Following the ludicrous outing, she had made up her mind
She was going to make him her own
Though he and I were already defined
She desperately wanted me to end up alone

I cried out to him that if he left with her it was over
She screamed out and called me horrid names
He stared blankly back at me as if we never loved
I could no longer take the piercing pain

I stumbled home pathetically
For this insanity was not even worth the fight
But the fact that the love of my life didn't bother to stand up for me
Is something that I will remember for the rest of my life

Warm Body

I convinced myself I loved you
Something frivolous, and that, I knew
But in you, I did find comfort
Though you were nothing but completely withdrew

Unconventional

Fitting in, I never did well
That I always knew
For I grew up quickly and aggressively
Because of everything I had been through

My Demise

Her destruction in the end
Hearts on sleeves she wore

Security

It's silly how just a few words
Make insecurity fade
But silence bring out fret
Even for just one day

Confidence

With open arms I accept
The manipulation and using of me
This is how I must think
Of I, myself, and me

Peer Pressure

"You have a flair for the dramatic"
They tell me more than often
And sometimes they do vocalize
My demeanor I should soften

Forgiveness

I never knew that I
Could say such awful things
For I had spent my life
A punching bag it seems

But you, your heart of gold
Forgiving like it beats
This is why I know
You are my necessity

Family

She's heard of a thing called freedom
Only vicariously
She lives her life in chains
Sheltered as a girl can be

What you thought was protection
Only drives away her most
You don't even know her
To you she's just a ghost

She feels the need to flee
For she knows she can't fight
Often does she visit
Her hidden secret life

What you wanted was sincere
A relationship first and foremost
But all that's under your roof
Are lies and theatrics of close

Prove Me Wrong

I wait for disappointment
It keeps me from living
But there's a reason why
Because they all keep leaving

Naïve

I knew that this was lust
Still I gave you my trust

You said all the wrong things
Still your words, they couldn't sting

You didn't hold the door
Still you shook me to my core

I told you I was done
Still it was you in the end who won

Runaways

We're good at pretending
We're not capable of feeling
But we gave in one night
And for that moment we knew of love
But when the morning came
We returned to routine
Running

I Honestly Don't Know

What is it about me?
Is it plastered on my face?
"Use me please," it says
"I'm just an open space"

They come and leave as pleased
For more than often so
Is it my disposition? I ask
When they didn't show

The Boy From Brittany

Why is it that we are at our happiest while saying goodbye?

What I Learned The Hard Way

Postpone anger
It is an unnecessary emotion
Patience is key, wait before you speak
Gossip is cheap, silence is golden

LOVE

'Love' comes from personal diaries of
learning to love others, and experiences
of both intimacy and heartbreak.

Shame

He asks about my past loves
Solemnly I bow my head
I hear words sputter from my mouth
Lying here in this bed

He stares innocently across from me
So safe he makes me feel
What would he ever think of me
If he knew my heart is made of steel

The truth? I think to myself
I don't know what love is
Nobody ever stayed
Nobody ever made me his

"Teach me," my eyes ask of him
As he holds on to my every word
"Don't worry," he blinks back silently
Maybe he will keep his word

Gentleman

How is it that you are real?
I watch your hand hold mine
For you speak like you've never hurt
I never saw the signs

It's the little things
That leave me out of breath
When you gaze into my eyes

Everything
Your cheeks when you smile
Even the way you said goodbye

Unfaithful

There was one night, still clear as day
I was lying next to you
The dark came, then politely you did
Ask me to sleep in the next room

And polite old me, nodded and smiled
For what more could I do
That cold, stiff couch hugged me that night
As I watched the lightning tumble through

Cheating

It seems it'd been forever
But him I finally met
Those emotionally abusive lovers
With him I finally forget

He's wonderful, kind, and true
His eyes electrifying blue
So why that when he sleeps
My mind cheats him with you

Relationship

It's like there's a pool table between us
A game between two people who don't know how to play
I'm all stripes and you're rock solid
We try our hardest not to give way

Sometimes we hit the other's cues
Accidentally hitting one can be fatal
So we maneuver around the dark
As long as we are able

It's entertaining, it's enjoyable
It's the back and forth
The give and take
For what it's worth

Young

I watched you telling stories
To the right of me
Before life taught us how to run
So innocent were we

You never held my hand
Never once asked for my heart
But we both knew that we
Could never be apart

Abandonment

You stare straight into me
Claiming that we feel right
I give into your eyes
For I completely lost my sight

You talked about her often
I guess I should have known
That you would leave me stranded
When she decided to make you her own

The Saddest Story Ever Told

I wasted my best shoes on you

What I Need You to Know

I know you feel rejection
I pushed you off of me
You stared confused and hurt
As we sat there silently

I hear you apologize
I try to find my words
My thoughts are blocking way
Of my vocal chords

We called it a mistake
Once the morning came
I didn't know how to tell you
I fall apart every time you say my name

I want you so damn bad
I think as I watch your back
Until you disappear
I know that you are what I lack

Why is it that we run?
When we're what the other needs
We'll meet again tonight
In my wildest dreams

Sleepless

In deep dreams I was one night
Frightened of those who left
Don't let him be like others I beg
"Don't let him, please" I said

I wake, for I feel eyes on me
They're yours, of sweet warm blue
I spend the rest of my night, watching you
Watching me, watch you

Courtesy

I know I have a mouth on me
I tend to speak my mind
There's nothing more attractive
Than when you put me in my place

We Can't Be Friends

You ask if we can meet
The same place we first met
Here we are sitting
Trying to forget

Strangers to one another
There's nothing left to say
You used to be haven
But now you are my biggest mistake

Freeloader

You needed the company
But you could never commit
You talked about the future
But the past you wouldn't forget

First Sight

It was electric
We politely shook hands
Your blue eyes beamed
Against your temping tan

I quickly walked away
Scared of what this was
You followed me around
I guess that's what attraction does

First Date

There you were, and so was I
Giddy and nervous and new
This is it, I thought as I
Smiled and walked towards you

For this could be our wonderful beginning
Or our horrific end
But you were radiant and honest
Trust. That, I was willing to lend

Our First Kiss

A moment is just a moment
Until you are swept away
I never understood those who gave up their freedom
That this was the reason they stayed

But you, you made me feel
More alive than I knew I could
And you, the way you felt
Just like my childhood

Today

Today was harder than others
We ended with our thumbs
There was nothing left but distance
I hadn't seen you in a month

My time had been spent waiting
Your secret hobby I'd become
My dignity was fading
I decided I was done

You said you wanted freedom
But are you really free?
When you can't spend one moment
Alone with your thoughts or with me

Your nights are wasted away
Surrounded by sweaty strangers
Does this really chase
Your quandaries and your dangers?

I could have been your escape
Held you when you cried
But all that's left of us
Is pathetic emptiness inside

Perfection

Every imperfection
Every insecurity
Every mistake
I have known and seen
But you are my definition of perfection

Faith

You are the reason I still believe
In an all-encompassing love

What Could Have Been

I see you are doing well
You have started dreaming again
Working hard
At everything you gave up on

I'm not going to lie
To myself and to you
That this doesn't get me stirring
Of words we exchanged when we were through

Polite

How are you
I'm good and you
That's all we know how to say

Something shifted
In our friendship
Ever since that day

Afraid of Alone

They want different things
They have never been defined
Why do they continue
If there is no finish line

Toxic

You still call, and I still answer
It's shameful, but it's true
For neither of us can stand the idea
Of a life without us two

Love

I discovered comfort one night
Your arms around me tight
Your heartbeat on my hand
You drew me in like quicksand

Home is how this feels
For I could never leave
Our hearts of when we were young
You are my sweet relief

I Miss You

I miss you
I miss your annoying habits
I miss your mess
You never seemed to see me at my best

But I miss your face
When I'd kiss you goodnight
And I'd never let us go to sleep
Until we resolved a fight

I miss our arguments
Gripping on to my phone
Tears streaming down
I'm on the floor all alone

But I knew as long and hard as we fought
It meant that I was still in your thoughts
Fighting means caring, right?
Or is that just something I was taught

It all started to fade away
Slowly day by day
We didn't seem to even notice
Until it just went away one day

I know you miss me too
But we seem to be pretty through
Because you hurt me and I hurt you
But you'll be stuck forever in my rear view

Your Eyes

Please don't look at me like that
The way that you do
Like a man deeply in love
If you don't intend to pursue

Me

"This is your fault," you say
I let myself think you are right
"Don't leave," I say
Self-pity for letting you make me feel this way

You silenced me without your hands
For reasons I can't explain
Why did you have this effect on me?
There's nobody else to blame

Ping Pong

Two different games
Round the world and backwards
One works out great each time
One hits downward leaving us shattered

We know how to love
And we know how to hate
Are we able to meet in the middle?
Or is it too little too late

Pulling Petals

He loves me when I'm always there
He loves me not, when I start to care

He loves the way I lend an ear
He hates when I talk about my fears

I love him when his guard comes down
But that's only when he decides to come around

YOUNG

'Young' is for everything else in the world; the extremities of the new generation, thoughts of a millennial, and everything in between.

The New Era

Things are different now
History is repeating itself
For they are naïve and ignorant
Their beliefs grown from collected dust on an antique shelf

Vanity

Oh sweetheart, don't you know
With your thick attitude
A life chasing after looks
Will never be beneficial to you

Yes, they call you beautiful
But they don't know your name
For it is those altered photographs
The reason behind your fame

Innovative

To be a creative
Is one of the most magical things a person can be
It is a gift; it is an offering
To those who cannot see

Delayed Flights

Parked on a frozen carousel
You and me, it was fate
Destiny brought us together
Our planes were both late

We didn't exchange names
But traded words for hours
Dancing around teenage butterflies
But then you mentioned something about her

The carousel started spinning
The world was no longer at pause
But that memory is a stamp in my passport
A place I visited and got lost

Intermission

Life needs to give me a fucking break

Grace Kelly

Two households, in fair Old Hollywood
Where we lay our scene
One a performer, full of grace. A superstar for the screen
The other a humble designer, of costumes for the elite

A passionate, forbidden love affair began
This love was one that even families couldn't come between
For money nor status mattered
When these two would convene

Enter a dashing Prince stage left
Now this character would intervene
For he had made the long journey from Monaco
In hopes of finding a maiden to introduce to the Queen

The humble designer was caught off guard
When his true love began to retreat
For the superstar was aggressively encouraged
For her and the Prince to arrange to meet

True love didn't win in this production
The superstar was swept gracefully off her feet
The Prince had found his Princess
And the humble designer admitted defeat

Concept

It's funny
The concept of company
The struggle between head and heart
Between need and want

Maturity

I know that I'm the one
Who said goodbye for good
But jabs right to my chest
Knowing you're in my neighborhood

I guess I'm growing up
Knowing what's best for me
But is it really best
If I miss you dreadfully?

Depressed

I know I am when I've stopped writing

Benjamin Button

Youth was so different

Unafraid of sharing
Caring
Loving

Here we are as unknowing adults

Afraid of what used to be like air
Doubtful
Scarred

Hayley N. Chow

"Will You Do My Homework?"

Growing up as an Asian American

How To Cut People Out Of Your Life

Politics

Best Friend

She wants the validation
She wants the money
She wants the house
She starts to shun me

So she'll take the ring
And the trips to Cabo
I lose the friend
I now call Jane Doe

Life Put Simply

Strangely enough
Life is about the calls you take
And the ones you don't

Free The Nipple

Take a seductive photograph
Post it on a square grid
Take it just for yourself
God forbid

She's asking for it
Trust me that they'll say
But as long as you feel beautiful
They don't matter anyway

Unfinished Poems

They are all about you

Elizabeth Taylor

Born into a life she didn't choose
Tossed around from lot to lot
Isn't she lucky? They'd say
At least that's what they thought

Draped herself in jewels
Shined like the star she became
A true queen she portrayed
In fact, she was a dame

And then there was him
A furious and passionate love
Together they were invincible
When push came to shove

Was she truly happy?
I guess we'll never know after her reign
But in the end she proudly proclaimed
She would have married him all over again

Quarantine

They cried and they ached
Begging for sunlight and air
These silly social characters
Drowning themselves in despair

But I meditated and I flourished
Took advantage of the time I was gifted
That when the untimely plague was over
I was shiny, new, uplifted

Swipe Left

To the ones who are an absolute bore
To the ones who never learned how to open the car door

To the ones who can't make up their minds
To the ones that are completely unkind

To the ones who are cheating
To the ones who are flighty and fleeting

To the ones who don't even bother
To the ones who don't appreciate a good author

Don't worry, I know I will be alright
And that one day I'll find Mr. Wonderfully Right

Rejection

They talk about relationships
But what they don't talk about is work
It's the new era, things are different now
Life simply doesn't come with perks

To Whom It May Concern

Life is tough
But you are tougher

Thank You

Words I don't say enough

Love Letter

Dear Hayley,

You have been to hell and back
Only to come out stronger
The woman you have always wanted to be
Well, you finally found her

Not once have you needed a man by your side
Never needed a running start
For you made your own dreams come true
Turned your life into living, breathing art

I hope that you have found true happiness
A peaceful state of mind

And I hope the opportunity comes when you
Inspire others to write a love letter to themselves too

CPSIA information can be obtained
at www.ICGtesting.com
Printed in the USA
LVHW052335090921
697444LV00001B/8